A Definitive Guide to

IPHONE 11
CAMERAS

A step-by-step Approach to taking Professional Photographs
and Shoot Cinematic Videos on iPhone 11 and 11 Pro Max

DERRICK
RICHARD

Copyright

Derrick Richard
ISBN: 9798631382336

ChurchGate Publishing House
USA | UK | Canada
© Churchgate Publishing House 2020

Contents

Who Needs This Book?

Are you finding iPhone photography and recording professional videos with your iPhone too technical? Or are you finding it difficult to get the right camera settings for that cinematic scene or crisp photographs? Maybe you just bought the iPhone 11 or 11 Pro, and need to learn about taking professional photographs and shoot some cinematic videos? Then this book is for you. The iPhone Camera looks simple on the surface, but when you dig deeper, you will realize it isn't that simple.

There are so many hidden camera features and settings that you probably don't know. This book will walk you through all you need to know about iPhone photography and shooting high-quality videos. You will be exposed to relevant iPhone camera settings and picking the correct values for each setting. The book will also help you understand each iPhone 11 and 11 Pro Max camera features and how to use each one of them in different photography and video recording scenarios. You will also find out how to shoot in different light conditions, different photography subjects, and different genres and styles of photography with pro apps like FiLMiC Pro.

At the end of this book, you should be able to understand iPhone photography and take the kind of photos or videos that nobody will believe were taken with the iPhone. You will also find a list of accessories that you would need to take your photography and video shoots to a whole new level.

Introduction

Apple released three iPhones in the iPhones 11 Series – The iPhone 11, iPhone 11 Pro and the iPhone 11 Pro Max. Apple focused on four major things for the new iPhone – the design, display, battery life and Cameras. The iPhone 11 Pro looks almost exactly like the iPhone XS from the front, although it is a little bit heavier and thicker. Except you are comparing them directly, you probably won't notice the difference in weight. You get a much bigger battery in exchange for that extra size which leads to a four hours battery life increase on a regular Pro and a five-hour jump for the Pro Max. However, the big difference from the iPhone XS is at the back of the phones. The rear glass for the iPhone 11 Series is now stronger and it comes in a frosted matt finish which does not pick up fingerprints. It also integrates a glossy Camera bump with triple Cameras on the 11 Pro Max and in contrast, the iPhone 11 has a dual camera setup. Images taken from the iPhone 11 series has far more improvement to that of the iPhone X. This improved picture quality is due to what Apple called Semantic Rendering. The Smart HDR recognizes what is in the image and renders it appropriately. This is how it works; firstly, the iPhone starts taking photos to buffer up the instance you open the camera App. By the time you press the camera button, it captures four underexposed frames of the photo, then it grabs one overexposed frame. This is basically what also happens in the iPhone X, but the difference is that the iPhone X does not capture the overexposed frame. Secondly, Smart HDR and Semantic Rendering looks for things in the photos it recognizes e.g., faces, hair, the sky, etc. Then it uses additional details from the underexposed and overexposed frames to selectively process the areas of the images it recognizes. Hairs get sharpened; the sky gets De-noised, faces gets retightened to make them look even. Smart HDR is also less aggressive in flattening the photos, and shadows are corrected to regain detail. Finally, the whole image is saved, and you have a photo. These all happens instantly every time you take a photo, which is a testament to how powerful the iPhone 11's processor is. The iPhone 11 is powered by an A13 Bionic Processor which is a far improvement of the iPhone X's A12 Bionic Processor in terms of Processing speed. There is also a new chip in the iPhone 11 called the U1, which does precise positioning using an ultra-wideband radio.

Physical Features of the iPhone 11

Front View

12 Megapixel
(Wide Camera)
F/1.8 Aperture
OIS Lens

Ambiant Light
Sensor

12 Megapixel
(Telephoto Camera)
F/2.4 Aperture
13MM Lens

Flash Light

Rear View of iPhone 11

12 Megapixel
(Wide Camera)
F/1.8 Aperture
OIS Lens

Ambiant Light
Sensor

12MP Ultra Wide Camera

Ambiant Light
Sensor

12 Megapixel
(Telephoto Camera)
F/2.4 Aperture
13MM Lens

Rear View of iPhone 11 Pro/11 Pro Max

4

The Display

The display of the iPhone 11 pro is the new OLED Super Retina XDR display. It runs from the top to the bottom with a notch at the top, rounded corners and uniform bezels. The significant upgrades on the screen are around brightness and power efficiency. The screen is now brighter than previous version of the iPhone and uses 50% less power. The color processing of the screen is so natural with Apple's tone system turned ON.

The Side Button

The side button of the iPhone 11 is at the top right-hand side of the phone. It is the most used button on the phones and the recommended grip on the phone is such that the index finger of your left hand easily rests over the side button. This makes for easy pressing of the button using the index finger of your left hand.

Volume Button

The volume buttons include the volume up at the top and volume down buttons below. The volume buttons is used in combination with other buttons for other functions besides increasing or decreasing sounds. Holding down the Volume down button for several seconds activates silent mode in the iPhone 11 and 11 Pro.

Rear Facing Cameras Features

At the back of the iPhone 11 Pro are three rear cameras and a flash. We have the wide, ultra-wide and telephoto cameras. The telephoto camera has the same basic sensor as that of the iPhone X but with a faster 52MM/F3.0 lens. The Wide Cameras are the same on the iPhone 11 and 11 Pro with the same F/1.8 lens and a slightly better sensor, while the New Ultra Wide Camera is twice as wide as the Wide Camera with an F/2.4 lens. The big difference is the telephoto lens. There is a clear distinction between the standard lens and the telephoto lens of the iPhone 11 cameras. The telephoto lens has two functions (1) to zoom in optically two times (2X) without losing the image quality. (2) to take portrait photos. The portrait mode allows you to have a sharp and crystal-clear focus on the primary subject and everything around the subject blurs out into a creamy background. This is known as Boca effect. With the Secondary Camera, you have five different modes to play around with – studio light, control light, stage light and Stage light monochrome.

You can select any of the three cameras to take photographs or record videos. The front-facing camera is also updated to record 4k videos at 24, 30 and 60 frames per second. Cameras on the iPhone 11 series have augmented reality improvements for objects with the ARKits technology. What this does is better detection of Objects in front and behind on the camera's frame.

There is also a new audio zoom feature that matches audio with the framing of your video, zooming in the videos and the sound generated by the object being recorded. The iPhone flash is 36% brighter than that of the iPhone X, XR and X Max.

Front Facing Camera Features

By the side of the front speaker is a 12MP front-facing Camera with an f/2.2 lens and a flash for taking wider-angle selfies and is cool for slofies (selfie in slow motion). The front facing camera has a wider lens of taking high quality wider images. With Apples update of the next generation smart HDR, the front facing camera can record 4K videos at 60 frames per second.

Understanding iPhone 11 Gestures

Tap

Briefly touch surface with the finger tips

Double Tap

Rapidly touch
surface twice with
finger tips

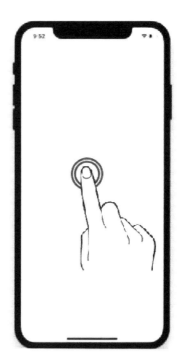

Haptic Touch

Formerly referred
to as 3D touch,
Haptic touch is
touching the surface
for an extended
period of time

Drag

Move finger over
the surface without
losing contact.

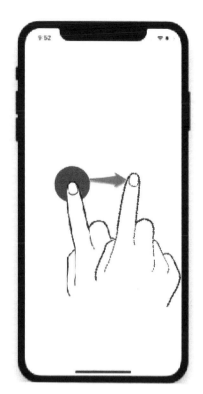

Pinch

Touch surface with
two or three
fingers and
bring them close
together

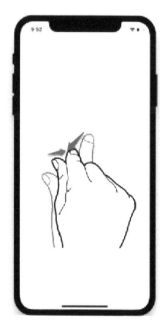

Spread

Touch surface with
two or three fingers
and move them
apart

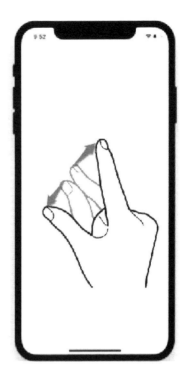

Swipe Up

Move finger tip
over surface from
bottom-up

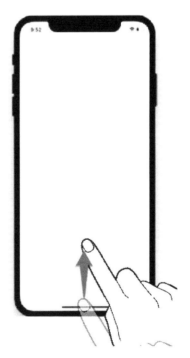

10

Swipe Down

Move finger tip
over surface from
top-down

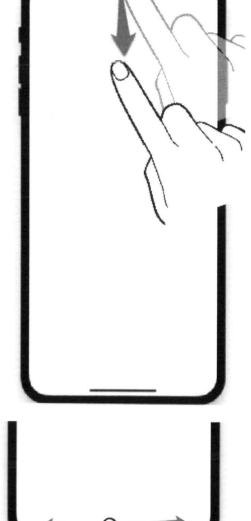

Swipe Side (Left

Swipe or Right

Swipe

Move Finger tip
on the surface to
either left or right.

11

Handy Photography and Video Accessories for the iPhone 11 Series

B efore we go into the tips and tricks of the iPhone camera app, let's look at some of the accessories you would need for that high-quality photo and video shoots. These access-ories are easy to find online, and they include - tripod, selfie ring light, 25x external telephoto lens, Motorized Slider, Gimbal, drone, lens protection cover, 8"/10.2" Dimmable Selfie Ring light, under-water photograph case, wide Angle 3-in-1 lens, Beastgrip, etc. We will now look at each of them in details.

Lens Protection Cover

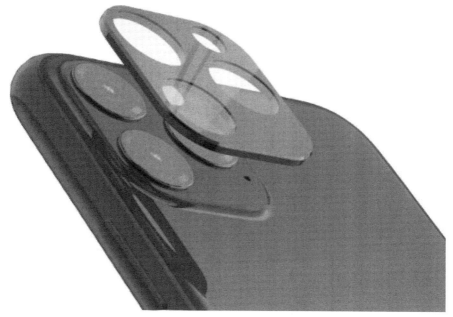

The Lens protective cover provides maximum protection for the iPhone 11 pro and pro max lens. It protects the cameras against fingerprints and scratch to maintain that quality photoshoot and high-resolution video shoot. The Lens Protection cover clips firmly to the cameras and does not easily fall off. This goes for less than $10 on amazon.com.

Profoto C1 Plus Flash

This is one accessory for those who wish to take their iPhone photography to a whole new level professionally. If you are tired of that wimpy flash that comes with your iPhone 11, then the Profoto C1 Plus Flash should be in your accessories kit. The Profoto is an external flash that can sync with your iPhone's camera. It requires a companion Profoto app to integrate properly to the iPhone 11 via Bluetooth. The Profoto Plus flash has some buttons on it to turn ON continuous lighting or adjust power output.

ROV Motorized Slider

This is an ideal accessory for panoramic video and photo shoots. You can set the start-point and end-point on the motorized slider to suit your cinematic video or professional photoshoots. The ROV motorized slider comes with multilevel adjustments, which give the cameras stability for more enhanced cinematic video shoots. It also comes with smartphone mounting clips, an 82mm lens clip, and a nice bag that keeps everything organized. The ROV slider is controlled with the ROV app, which can be downloaded from the app stores. You can adjust the speed and direction of the slider plus time lapse settings. The ROV battery life is excellent and lasts up to 24 hours on a good day but consistently hovers between 22 hours, which is still very good. The battery status is seen at the LED lights next to the power button.

Fuji Instax SP3 Printer

This is a battery-powered portable printer, which is a little bit bigger than the iPhone 11 Pro Max, making it perfect for tossing into the bag. It prints high-quality Polaroid styled square photographs, which have plenty of detail in color in a matter of seconds. The iPhone syncs to the Fuji Instax Sp3 printer via the Fuji App.

Handheld Gimbal Stabilizer

The handheld gimbal stabilizer is an ideal accessory that keeps your footage stable. It features an integrated control panel design, a focus pull, zoom capability with improved camera balance, anti-shake plus auto adaptation capabilities. The handheld gimbal stabilizer supports instant scene transition for that smooth filming experience. It is powered by a 4000mAh battery, which is durable enough to power your cinematic filmmaking workflow.

25x External Telephoto Zoom Lens

This allows users to increase the zoom rate of the telephoto lens by 25x, zooming in objects at a distance 20 times with a magnificent close-up shot. With the 25x External telephoto zoom lens, distance is no obstacle to that great photo you wish to take. The external telephoto lens is easy to attach and use on the iPhone 11 and 11 Pro.

Wide Angle 3-in-1 lens

The wide-angle 3-in-1 lens is a professional lens that enhances clarity and best quality when shooting cinematic videos on your iPhone 11 or 11 Pro. The 3-in-1 wide-angle lens provides an improved shooting distance and reduces wide-angle lens distortions. It is easy to mount on the iPhone 11 and provides more stable imagery. This lens also goes for less than $40 on amazon.

Rode VideoMiC Me-L

If you desire a portable and easy-to-use external microphone for your video shoots, outdoor film making, vlogging, Instagram story, or any occasion where you need to capture higher quality audio on the iPhone 11, 11 Pro and 11 Pro Max, then the Rode Video-Mic Me-L is what you need. This is connected to the lightning port of the iPhone.

SANDMARC Hybrid Filters

These Hybrid filters from SANDMARC combine the depth of field and control shutter speed of any filters with the vibrant colors and contrast of pure filter.

With this, landscape photography and outdoor film making get a more cinematic look. By protecting the camera from overexposure and improving the dynamic range, the hybrid filter gives you the highest possible control of your camera plus a well-distributed and balanced tint.

Adonit Photogrip QI

This allows you to transform your iPhone into a camcorder or a digital camera. To top up that camera experience with the photo-grip, it comes with a detachable Bluetooth connected shutter button at the top to give it that digital camera feel. Combined with a tripod, you can take selfies without having to set up camera timers on the phone. The tripod can also serve as a second handle for that extra steady photo or video shoot.

Beastgrip

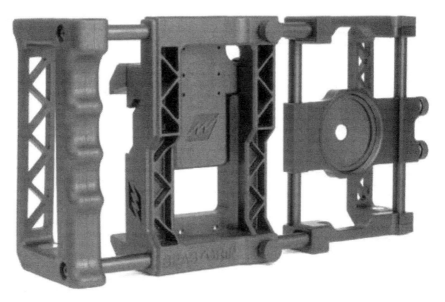

The beastgrip allows you to mount a full-frame camera lens on to your iPhone 11. This takes your photography or cinematic videos to a whole new level giving it a depth of field and extra dynamism. You can also attach the beatgrip to a remotely controlled motorized slider. This makes you do things like time lapses or add a bit of motion to your recording. Another accessory you can attach to the iPhone via the beastgrip is the spotlight. Spotlights are made for DSLR cameras, but with the beastgrip, it can be attached to the iPhone 11.

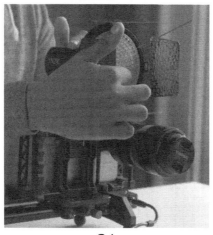

Note that you need a DOF adapter and some pro software like the FilMic Pro installed on your iPhone to be able to add all these accessories connected to the beastgrip to sync to your iPhone. We will discuss the FiLMi Pro later in the manual.

The beastgrip also has provisions for attaching a variety of lenses that can pull focus while shooting from the background to the foreground or verse versa. Also, the spotlight mounted on the beastgrip comes with a low light performance switch, which results in sustained crisp photographs.

Lumu Power Light Meter

If you struggle with white balancing on your smartphone photo-graphy or video recording, then you need the Luma Power Light Meter. This device takes away the headaches associated with getting the proper setting. You simply plug it into your lightning port on your iPhone. Install the Lumu white balancing app, which can be downloaded from the App's Store. With the app, you have a professional balance color meter and exposure meter. To get the proper white balance setting, point the Lumu sensor to an object or scene, and jot down the readings. Then go into the FiLMiC Pro app if you have one or if you are using a dedicated camera, go to your white balance settings and input the color temperature and tint values you got from the Lumu app.

Dimmable Selfie light with tripod

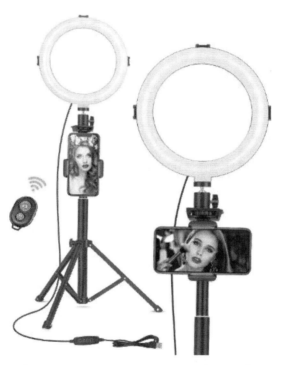

The dimmable selfie light provides cool lighting for selfies photos and filming in dark scenery or an environment with poor illumination. It comes with a tripod stand that holds your iPhone in place while bringing more brightness to image. The tripod can be adjusted to different angles when making videos on your iPhone 11. The dimmable selfie light can also be controlled via wireless remote, and the light is powered via a USB cable. This stand comes in 8" and 10.2" rings and is available on www.amazon.com for less than $30.

Underwater Photograph case

Taking professional underwater photographs requires a level of protection for your iPhone 11 and 11 pro. This case is IPX8 certified, which means it can survive photo shoots or video recording at a depth of 15meters or 50 feet with high-quality underwater camera performance. So if you are looking for a case that will protect your iPhone while you record that swimming, kayaking, boating, or any other water activities, then the under-water photograph case is your best bet. The underwater photo-graph case can easily be screwed to a tripod or gimbal. This accessory is available on amazon.com for less than $40.

Tripod

This is used to capture moments with friends and family or shoot professional videos. They are also ideal for selfies and can be adjusted to the best angle you want. Tripods allow you to capture more scenery, unlike when you take images with the phone in your hands. This is a portable device because it can be adjusted to fit into any small bag making it easy to move around. Most tripods go for less than $30 on Amazon.

Getting the Right Camera Settings

Except you get the camera settings right, you won't get the highest quality photographs or videos. So in this section, we will have a walkthrough of all the important iPhone 11 camera settings and the right values for each setting if that crisp photograph is your target.

- Tap on 'Settings' on the home screen

- Scroll down until you find 'Camera' and select it.

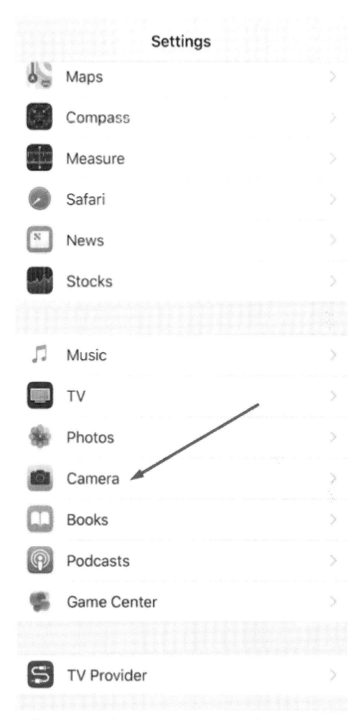

Settings

	Maps	>
	Compass	>
	Measure	>
	Safari	>
	News	>
	Stocks	>
	Music	>
	TV	>
	Photos	>
	Camera	>
	Books	>
	Podcasts	>
	Game Center	>
	TV Provider	>

- This will open up the 'Camera Settings'

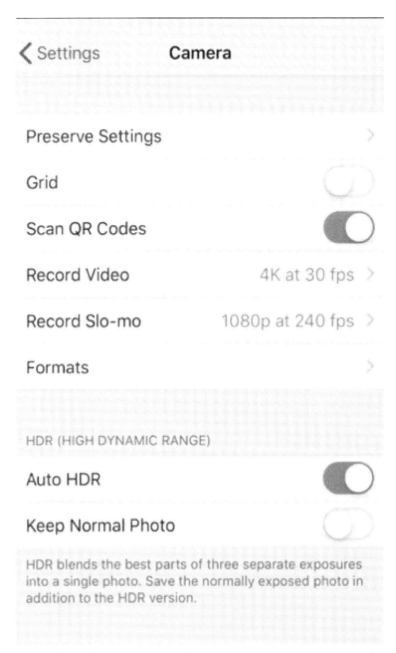

Preserve Settings ❯

Grid

Scan QR Codes

Record Video　　　4K at 30 fps ❯

Record Slo-mo　　1080p at 240 fps ❯

Formats ❯

HDR (HIGH DYNAMIC RANGE)

Auto HDR

Keep Normal Photo

HDR blends the best parts of three separate exposures into a single photo. Save the normally exposed photo in addition to the HDR version.

• Here, the first option that is very important is the Grid Settings. The Grid is turned OFF by default. Toggle ON the Grid view and when the camera app is launched you will find two horizontal and two vertical grid lines on the viewfinder.

Grid

These grid lines are useful when composing your shots.

- The next important setting is the Format option. Tap on 'Format'

Formats   ›

This brings up two camera capture options you can choose from - 'High Efficiency' and 'Most Compatible' image file format.

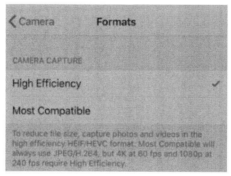

High efficiency corresponds to the 'HEIF image file format' while most compatible corresponds to the 'JPEG file format.' High efficiency is a file format that is mostly used by Apple, while most compatible or JPEG is the most popular image file format in the world. If you don't know what these acronyms mean, don't worry; just ensure you select the Most Compatible Option. The benefit of high efficiency is that your photographs will take up less storage space, but Most Compatible has two very substantial benefits. In essence, the files are more compatible across devices, especially if you are sending them over to your friends who do not use Apple

31

devices. The second benefit is the fact that most compatible images are of higher quality with more detail.

- At the bottom of the Camera Settings screen, you will find
HDR settings.

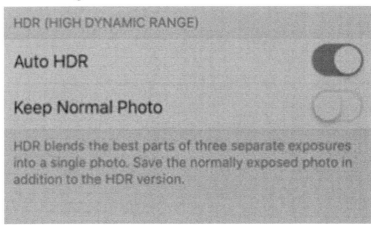

To take full control of your cameras, turn OFF the 'Auto HDR' and
the 'Keep Normal Photo' option should be turned ON.

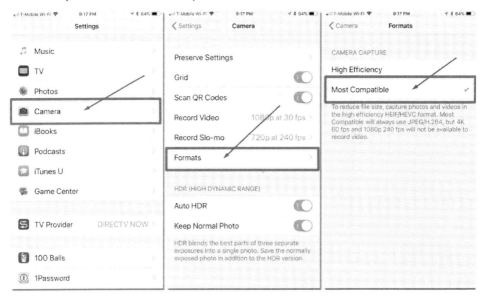

Basic iPhone 11 Camera Functions

The Camera Viewfinder Interface

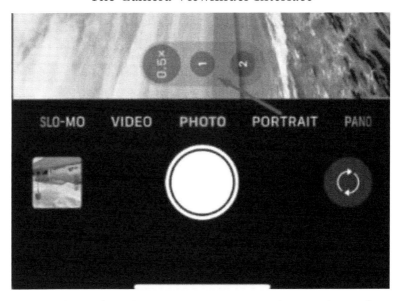

The user interface for the iPhone 11 is similar to that of previous iPhones but with some little variations. You can switch between the ultra-wide, telephoto, and wide-angle lens by tapping on 0.5x, 1, and 2, respectively.

To capture an image,

- · Focus your camera on the image,

- · Select the lens you want and

- · tap on the shutter button ⬤ or press the volume button

Taking Photographs in burst mode

Taking photographs in burst mode means taking several pictures in quick succession.

- Focus your phone on the target object

- Slide the shutter to the left, and it takes several frames of your image.

Night Mode

The iPhone 11 and 11 Pro both have a night mode, which provides users with super low light high-quality photography. It doesn't only take a more prolonged exposure, but combines multiple exposures and uses these different photos to reduce any noise automatically. In other words, it chooses an exposure that it thinks is best for your image. It determines the exposure based on how much movement is in the scene and how much light is available.

By default, as soon as you launch the camera app in a low ight environment, the night mode will automatically be enabled. Make sure you have your flash disabled for night mode to be effective.

A night mode photograph of Berlin Brandenburg gate

To disable the flash, tap on the flash icon at the top left corner of the camera app, and the night mode icon  turns yellow.

Next, keep the night mode at the default auto mode, and while holding your phone still, tap on the shutter button to take your photographs. For a better night mode photograph result, place the iPhone on a tripod and set the timer to three seconds.

More Access to Your Camera Features

At the top of the viewfinder is a grayed out arrow ⌃ ,which, when tapped gives you access to different options on the camera. For instance, you have a shortcut for the flash ⚡, live photo ⊚ , aspect ratio **4:3**, shutter timer⟳ and filters ●.

Applying Filters

To apply filters to your photograph, place your iPhone in land-scape and the camera App. At the top-left corner of the Camera app is the greyed out filter icon◼. When you tap on the filter icon, the filter menu opens up. Now, swipe through the different filter options such as vivid cool, vivid warm, dramatic, etc and select anyone suitable for your photograph or video. You can go back to the original image without filters by swiping back and tapping on 'Original' on the filter menu. You can tell that one of the filter options is activated if the filter icon changes from grey to color ●.

Every time the filter icon is in color, a filter has been activated. Exit the filter menu by tapping the filter icon again. If you don't want to use filters, there are other steps you can take to improve the quality of your images in post-processing.

Setting up Self Timer

The self-timer allows you to set the camera to take a photograph after a stipulated time. Let's say you wish to take a family portrait, and you don't want any member of the family to miss out on the moment. Instead of making any member of the family, the photo-grapher, you could set the camera on a tripod and set the timer to give you ample time to join them up in the photograph. To activate the self-timer, click on the self-timer icon on the camera app menu. You can either switch the Self-timer Off or set it to 3 seconds or 10 seconds.

Live Photos

The live video functionality records videos before and after a picture you take. The general guideline is to keep live photos ON every time there is movement in the scene or whenever you are taking pictures of people. The live photo icon turns yellow when it is turned ON.

HDR

iPhone 11 has a High Dynamic Range imaging - a feature that helps fix photographic errors and makes photographs look appealing. HDR is ideal when taking casual pictures. You also have the option to turn HDR ON/OFF or set in AUTO mode from the camera app. It is recommended to set HDR to Auto.

Flash

This is used in activating the camera flash if you wish to take flash photography. You have the option to turn it ON, OFF, or leave it at AUTO. However, the best recommendation in smartphone photography is to keep the flash OFF. This is because the flash on the iPhone is relatively weak. It only works well when your subject is very close, and even then, you may end up with unnatural looking colors and other potential image quality problems. Because of this, it is better to leave the flash off, else get an external flash with a higher resolution like the Profoto C1 Plus

Flash. But for most photography situations, even in low light, it is recommended that you keep the flash OFF.

Switching between Front Facing and Rear Facing Cameras

The 12 megapixels (f/2.2 Aperture) front-facing camera, also known as the selfie or slofie camera, shoots 1080 pixel videos at 120 frames per second, slow-motion 4k videos at 24, 30 and 60 frames per second. The front-facing camera is toggled ON by tapping the camera flip icon ◙ next to the shutter button. It is ideal to place the phone in landscape when taking selfies. This is because in landscape, the camera is shooting at 12MP, but in portrait, it goes down to 7MP. When the phone is placed in portrait, you will observe that the camera zooms in and zooms out a bit when it is placed in landscape. For the best resolution result, leave it at landscape when taking selfies or slofies.

While the phone positioned in landscape, you can carryout different settings on the camera. For instance, you can turn ON the live photo mode by tapping on the live photo icon ◎ on the top left corner. You can also add filters to the image by tapping on the filter ⬤ button next to the live photo button. Other settings you can apply including setting up a timer, turn flash ON/OFF etc.

Switching Between Cameras

You can switch between the three cameras on the iPhone 11 Pro Max from the viewfinder. Tapping on the 1x switches the camera mode to the Wide, 0.5x for the Ultra Wide, and 2x for the telephoto camera.

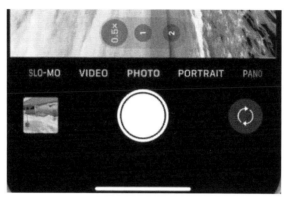

Wide Camera   *Ultra Wide*

You can be creative and get some beautiful shots if you get the right angle with the wide and ultra-wide cameras on the iPhone 11. However, if you don't select the right lens for your photoshoot, the iPhone automatically does that. It chooses a camera ideal for the photograph it finds in the viewfinder. This is made possible by the inbuilt new autofocus face detection technology built into the iPhone 11's cameras.

You can take some beautiful close up shots from any of the cameras automatically selected by the iPhone. To do this, tap on the viewfinder, set the focus on the object, then lock the camera on autofocus by tapping and holding on the viewfinder. Finally, tap on the shutter button.

Ultra Wide Shot

With the camera locked on autofocus, you can adjust brightness by simply swiping up or down.

Zooming in On Images

You can zoom in or out on objects by pinching in or out on the viewfinder. However, to get that ideal zoom spot for objects, tap and hold the wide camera 1x spot on the viewfinder until the zoom wheel pops up. Rotate the zoom wheel to the left or right to zoom in or out on the object on the viewfinder. This feature does a great job of transitioning from the different lenses while the zoom wheel is rotated.

Taking Live Photos

When photographs are taken with 'Live photo' enabled, you can preview or re-live the moment the photo was taken by going into your library, and tap on the image for one or two seconds. The photograph is played like a little video clip. One aspect where live photo feature is useful is when taking a group photo and discover that someone in the photograph blinked, you can edit the image by simply tapping on 'Edit' and move the slider to the part of that clip where everyone's eyes are open and then use that as the main photograph. With this feature enabled, you don't have to retake that photograph.

Taking Slofies

Slofies are slow motion selfies of yourself taken with front-facing camera. Before taking Slofies, you must set your cameras to record your slofies between 1080p HD at 120fps or 1080p HD at 240fps. Go to settings > Camera > Record Slo-Mo and select between these options.

Now, to take slofies;

- Open the camera app
- Tap the camera flip icon 🔄 to switch from the rear-facing camera to your front-facing camera
- Swipe through the shooting options above the shutter button and choose Slo-mo.
- When you're ready, tap the red shutter button to start your slow-motion video. Tap the button again to stop.
- Your slofie will be automatically saved to your Camera Roll.

Setting up Composition

Setting up compositions to capture photos or videos outside the frame will capture other objects or subjects which are not in focus with the ultra-wide lens focusing on images outside the focus. In contrast, the telephoto or wide lens focuses on your object or subject. This way, you can increase the captured frame and make

44

objects at the background visible. To toggle ON composition settings, tap on settings > camera > scroll down to 'Composition' and toggle ON 'Photos Capture Outside the Frame,' 'Videos Capture Outside the Frame' and 'Auto Apply Adjustments.' When 'photos capture outside the frame' option is enabled, it captures two photos together, one with your current lens and the other with the lens zoomed out a bit. It captures these two photos and overlays them to produce a high-quality image.

This is awesome because, let's say, for example, you took a photo, and the subject you are trying to get within the frame is out of frame. Since you have the 'Photos Capture Outside the Frame' enabled, you can go into your photo library, tap 'Edit.'

- Click on the ellipses at the top right

- Tap on 'Use content outside frame'

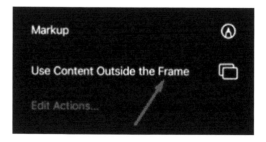

- This brings up a more extensive field of view from that photo. So there is no need to retake photos, especially when it has to do with capturing moments that cannot be repeated. You can do same on videos as well.

Images capture is composition mode takes up more storage and would be automatically deleted within thirty days. So you have thirty days to use such images.

Camera Modes of the iPhone 11

There are several camera modes on the iPhone 11. You can switch between these different photo and video modes by swiping vertically on the viewfinder screen. The modes include Photo mode, square mode, Video Mode, Portrait mode, Panorama Mode, Portrait Mode, SLO-MO and TIME-LAPSE Mode.

Portrait Mode

Portrait mode is used to take images in a beautifully blurred out background. This mode is designed to take high-quality photographs of pets and other subjects with several advanced photography options. You take different photos by switching between the telephoto lens, wide and ultra-wide lens in the portrait mode. The portrait mode option is also fully supported on the front-facing camera. Several lighting effects can be applied to subjects in the portrait mode, and this includes contour light, natural light, studio light, stage light, etc. The 'stage light' effect places objects within a stage light while the 'studio light' and 'natural light' effect place subjects within 8 feet of the camera.

Pano Mode

The pano or panorama mode allows you to capture a lot more photos in one shot. To capture images in the panorama mode, move the viewfinder across a wide area you wish to capture with the iPhone Camera set to the ultra-wide.

Square Mode

The square mode is just like the regular photo mode, but this time, they are only taking square photos. What happens here is that the iPhone crops your pictures before they are taken. When you take a square photo, there is nothing you can do to expand it to the full-sized picture. But if a regular wide photo is taken, it is easy to crop that into a square.

SLO-MO Mode

This is used for shooting super slow-motion videos.

Time Lapse Mode

Time lapse videos are essentially the opposite of SLO-MO videos. Time lapse videos move very fast.

Aspect Ratio

Apple gives you several aspect ratios to choose from on the iPhone 11. The 16:9 is the standard aspect ratio. However, you can select between 4:3, square and 16:9

The Photo app shows you all of the photographs you have taken with your phone. Starting with the "Photos tab", it is a great way to get a high or low-level overview of your photos. In the photo's app, there are the "days," "months," "years," and the "All photos" section. This allows you to adjust your search or view based on what image you are looking for and when they were taken. The cool thing about "Days" is that it highlights the important photosand arranges them chronologically.

The "All photos" allows you to view all the photos you have taken. You can zoom-in on the photos by tapping on the ellipses at the top right corner, then tap on the plus symbol or Zoom-out by tapping on the minus symbol.

In the Photos app, videos and live photos automatically playback making the photos feel very much alive. To activate auto-play videos and live photos,
- go to "Settings"
- tap "Messages"
- tap "photos"
- toggle ON "Auto Videos and Live Photos."

Tap on a photo to enter edit mode. In edit mode, you could pinch to zoom to get up close and personal to see those details, add filters and also adjust the intensity of filters to photos.

The "vibrance enhancement" allow you to boost colors without affecting skin tones.

You can also fine-tune white balance by adjusting the Warmth & Tint balance.

Sharpen tool allow you to make edges in your photos crisper and better refined. The "Definition" tool allows you to adjust image clarity while the "Noise Reduction" tool allows you to reduce or eliminate graininess and speckles within your photos.

Vignette adds shadings to the edges of your photos to make your subject stand out. Note that you can review each of these effects individually. You can turn these effects ON or OFF by simply tapping on their icons.

Another addition to the photo editor is the "Portrait Lighting Control." The Portrait Lighting Control adjusts the position and intensity of each Portrait Lighting effect. So you can easily sharpen eyes or brighten and smooth facial features just like a photographer would in a photo studio.

Shooting Videos On the iPhone 11

efore going into details on how to shoot and professional videos with the iPhone 11, you need to know some basic terms to help you understand the section. Some of the terms include – white balance, shutter speed, ISO, and frame per second.

White Balance

White balance in video recording is a process of removing unrealistic color casts so that images that appear white in real life also appear white in your video or photo. Proper lens white balance takes cognizance of the color temperature of the light source for the video.

Frame Rate Per Second (fps)

This is the speed at which images in a video are shown. A better illustration is when you flip through a book. The faster the flip through, the higher the frame rate. So if a video is captured and played back at 30fps, that means each second of the video shows 30 distinct still images. In other words, frame rate is the individual frame that comprises each second of a video. For example, a camera shooting at "4K 30 fps" means we have a new image with a resolution of 3840x2160 displayed 30 times per second. While a camera recording at "4K 60 fps" displays twice as many images in the same amount of time, thus requiring more powerful hardware to do it. Higher fps means smoother motion in the video. Higher resolution means more detail in each frame.

Shutter Speed

Shutter speed is how long an individual frame is exposed to light. It is sometimes confused with frame per second. However, they are different. The shutter speed determines the amount of motion blur in each frame of your video. For example, when shooting at 25fps, your shutter speed should be 1/50 of a second. If your camera can shoot at 50 or 60 fps, your shutter speed should be 1/100 or 1/125 of a second.

ISO

ISO has to do with the level of sensitivity of your camera to the available light. The lower the ISO of a camera, the less sensitive it is, while a camera with higher ISO has a higher sensitivity to light. It is recommended that you stick to the lowest or base ISO of your camera when shooting videos in an area where there is more light to minimize the appearance of noise on your footage. The base ISO is typically 100 or 200. The higher the ISO, the more noise creeps into your footage.

You can record a video on your iPhone by tapping on 'Video from the camera menu or by pressing and holding the shutter button (the big white button at the center of the camera interface) until it turns red (record button). To lock the phone in record mode, slide the little recorder button to the right🔒. This leaves the record button at the center and the shutter button to the right.

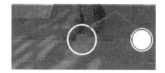

When you tap on the shutter button while the phone is still in video record mode, it takes a photograph amidst the video recording. Like in camera mode, you can also switch between the wide, ultra-wide, and telephoto lenses when recording videos. The iPhone 11 is capable of shooting 4K videos at 24, 30 and 60 frames per second and slow-motion videos at 120 and 240 frames per second. 4k 30fps videos are amazingly stable, thanks to optical image stabilization and software stabilization working together on the iPhone 11. When shooting in low light, the phone automatically switches frame rates from 30fps to 24fps, so each frame is exposed for a slightly longer time and captures more light to make the video look good. 4K 60fps videos are very stable from the primary camera, but in contrast, shooting 4k 60fps videos on the Wide-angle lens does not have optical image stabilization. However, it still produces some amazing video footage. You can seamlessly switch between these lenses while shooting videos if you are recording at 30fps. But, if you are shooting at 4K 60fps, you will need to choose the lens you want to record with before you hit the record button. But this can be achieved using apps like the FiLMiC Pro.

How to Configure Filming Speed On the iPhone

Whether you are a fan of shooting videos with that smooth 60 frames per second motion at 1080p or the super smooth 24 frames per second at 4K, the iPhone 11 has your back. To configure your filming speed, go to "Settings" > tap "Camera" > Select "Record Video" and choose from the list of filming speeds.

FiLMiC Pro for Cinematic Video Recording

If you are willing to get the most out of your iPhone's video capabilities, then you need to download FiLMiC Pro for $15. It is packed with several features, which unlocks DSLR-like settings on your iPhone 11 Camera. FiLMiC Pro is one app that allows you to record videos from all four cameras at the same time. It gives you full manual control of your shutter speed, focus, frames per second, white balance, ISO, etc. You also get LOG V2 with the FiLMiC Pro, which, according to the developers, gives you up to 2.5 stops of additional dynamic range, which exceeds some DSLR cameras.

Setting Up FiLMiC Pro

Learning how to operate and capturing great shots on the FiL-MiC Pro app comes down to a lot of experimentation and practice. Here, we will walk you through the FiLMiC pro interface and some tips and tricks to get you started.

Main Menu

To access the settings menu of the FiLMiC Pro, click on the settings icon at the lower-left corner to open up the main menu.

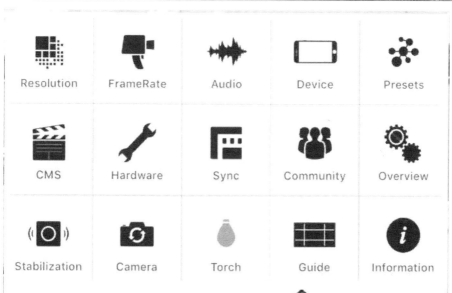

Now, we will take the menu items one after the other to explain how each one of them works. We will also look at some ideal settings to help you with your video shoot.

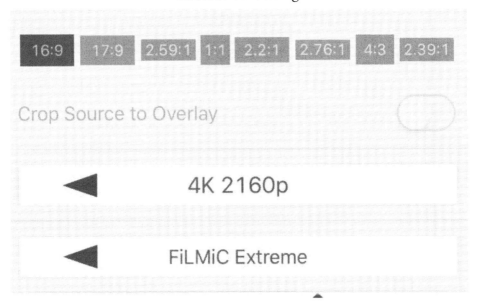

The first thing you need to do when using the filmic pro app is to decide your recording resolution. The resolution is the quality of the files you will be capturing. Click on the 'Resolution' tab to open up the settings. The first thing you will notice is the different aspect ratios across the top. 16:9 is the standard aspect ratio for shooting cinematic or any other professional videos. Choosing a different aspect ratio other than 16:9 will turn ON "Crop Source to Overlay." It is recommended that you turn this OFF. Turning it OFF will still give you the framing guide for your chosen aspect ratio and also record the full image area outside the guides. This will give you the ability to adjust your framing later on. However, the recommended aspect ratio for Instagram filming is 1:1.

Next, you want to select your resolution. The recommended resolution is 2160p at 4K, which gives you a higher quality video but will take up a lot of storage space.

Below the resolution setting, you have the menu to choose the bit rate or recording quality. This directly determines the recording bit rate, and it is important to set this as high as possible. There are four options to choose from - FiLMiC Extreme, Economy, Apple Standard, and FiLMiC Extreme. 'Economy' is the lowest quality setting, while FiLMiC Extreme is the best quality the Apps provides. The FiLMiC Extreme gives you much better and more quality video settings than the built-in iPhone 11 camera app offers. So if you have the storage space available and you want the best quality recording out of your phone's camera, then you want to set it at FiLMiC Extreme. For the Video Codec, HEVC is the ideal option.

Next you want to select your resolution. The recommendation resolution is 2160p at 4K in most situations for later post processing. This gives you a higher quality video but will take up a lot of storage space. One good reason to choose a lower resolution is if you want to use high frame rate to record slow motion. Below the resolution setting you have the menu to choose the bit rate or recording quality. This directly determines the recording bit rate and it is important to set this as high as possible. There are four options to choose from - FiLMiC Extreme, Economy, Apple

Standard, and FiLMiC Extreme. Economy is the lowest quality setting and FiLMiC Extreme is the best quality the Apps provides. The FiLMiC Extreme gives you a much better quality videos than the built-in iPhone 11 camera app will on your phone. So if you have the storage space available and you want the best quality recording out of your phone's camera, then you want to be using EiLMiC Extreme. For the Video Codec, HEVC is the ideal option.

FrameRate Settings

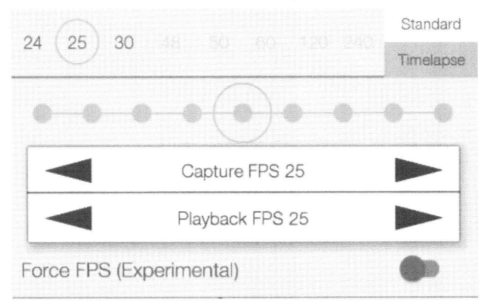

This is used to edit, capture, and playback frame rate. This is very useful for cinematic effect, and it gives that little bit of motion blur and a bit of realism to the film you get. The default is 24 frames per second, capture, and playback. But you can select any frame rate available for your chosen resolution. You will notice that the 48, 50, 60, 120, and 240 framerates are greyed out. But if we change the resolution and recording quality, they will be activated. Anything above 30fps is cast as slow motion. So for most videos, you will be creating, you would need to use one of the active framerates (24,25 and 30). Stick to 30 frames per second if you are in the United States, but if you are in Australia or Europe, set your frame rate to 25fps. This will help you remove or reduce the chance of any flickering happening from any lights that are in your scene. After selecting your ideal framerate, tap on anywhere on the screen to go back to the previous menu.

Audio Settings

Tap on audio to open audio settings. You can select your micro-phone source from here. You decide if you want to use the iPhone's inbuilt microphone or an external microphone plugged into the iPhone for better quality sound. When an external microphone is attached to the iPhone, it pops up in the audio setting option. Turning ON 'Video Only' will allow you to record without audio. You also have the opportunity to choose between different sound qualities, but the recommended audio quality is 48.0kHz

Device Settings

Save To Camera Roll

Enable Remote

Orientation Lock

Stitch Recorded Footage

Tap on 'Device' to open device settings. Here you can enable remote control if FiLMiC Remote is linked to your FiLMiC Pro (FiLMiC Remote will be explained later on in this section). You could also toggle ON orientation Lock to put the video locked to either portrait or landscape mode. Orientation lock prevents the rotation of your screen when you rotate your device.

Toggle ON 'Save to Camera Roll' to be able to save video clips to the Camera Roll. Toggle ON 'Stitch Recorded Footage' to shoot multiple videos and automatically join them together. This allows

62

for in-camera editing without having to use a separate editing app.

How to save from FiLMiC Pro to the Camera Roll

1. Tap to open the FiLMiC Library.

2. Tap the multi-clip selector button.

3. Tap each clip you want to save to the Camera Roll to add it to the selection (turns green)

4. Tap the Save to Camera Roll button.

5. Your clips will be copied to the Photos app.

6. Wait until all selected clips turn red which indicates the transfer has completed.

Presets

Reset to Default Settings

4K 24fps 100Mbps ✓

Save Current Settings as Preset

Tap on preset to save your settings so you can quickly call them up later or while recording video clips or taking photographs.

You can have different presets, for instance, you can have a setting for 1080p and another for 4k and switch between these settings during video shoots or photography depending on what you intend to achieve with your recording.

Content Management System (CMS)

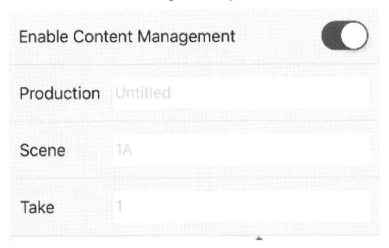

The Content Management System settings panel is where you name your media.

Hardware

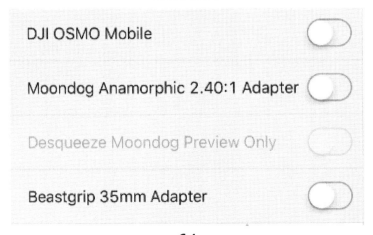

The Hardware settings enable FiLMiC Pro to be used with various external hardware options such as the DJI OSMO Mobile, Moondog Anamorphic adapter, Beastgrip adapter, COVR Photo Lens etc.

Sync

The FiLMiC Sync enables you to sync your presets to a Cloud storage account, allowing you to apply them easily to multiple devices.

Community

Tap on the 'community' to find all the ways you can connect to FiLMiC Pro on social media.

Overview

Active preset: 4K 24fps 100Mbps

3840X2160 @ FiLMiC Extreme

24FPS / 24FPS

Video Only

No Active Hardware Solutions

If you wish to see a summary of all your settings on the FiLMiC Pro app, tap on 'Overview.'

Stabilization

Stabilization is very important when shooting videos on the iPhone. To turn ON/OFF optical image stabilization depending on your needs, tap on 'Stabilization.'

Camera Settings

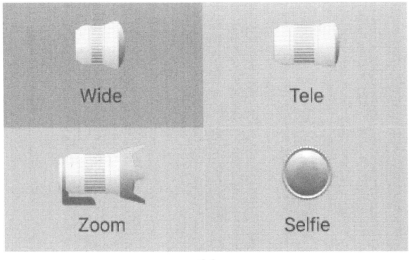

Whether it is the front-facing or rear-facing cameras or an external camera attached to the iPhone, it is easy to switch between
these cameras on the FiLMiC Pro App but tapping on 'Camera'
on the Settings Menu.

Guide

The Guide settings is used for turning ON or OFF gridlines on the
viewfinder.

Information

Quick Start Guide

Tutorials

Support Page

Version   6.1.2 (Build 762)

Tap on tutorials to find links to more tutorials to aid you in
mastering the FiLMiC Pro App. Here, you can also find the current
version of FiLMiC Pro installed on your iPhone.

Exposure and Focus Assist

With FiLMiC Pro app now set up on your iPhone, let's look at the
image analysis tools provided by FiLMiC Pro to assist with expo-

sure and focus. Now, tap on the 'A' icon at the bottom left corner of the screen.

This brings up the live analytics at the top of the screen.

The Zebra cross overlay ▨ shows areas of overexposure with red stripes. While the Flipping overlay ▨ indicates the area of the image which are extremly under or overexposed. The false color overlay ◉ is useful when judging overall exposure. The green areas your see on the screen are within proper exposure range. The focus picking overlay FP indicates objects in focus with a blue outline and areas of critical focusing are shown in green color.

Filmic Pro provides Live instagram waveform monitors, cycle thro-ugh them by tapping on time code area to cycle between luminous Instagram, RGB Instagram and waveform.

Setting White Balance

Before recording anything, you need to make sure your white balance is set correctly. To set the white balance, tap the colored circles 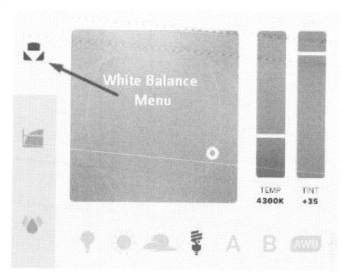 at the bottom left part of the screen to open the imaging panel.

In the Temperature tab of the imaging panel, you will find complete manual control of your white balance. You can use the metrics to select any temperature and tint value in the range. Just move the slider to choose the right color temperature and tint. The white balance preset gives you a good starting point for shooting under Tungsten, Candescent light, sunlight, overcast light, and fluorescent lighting.

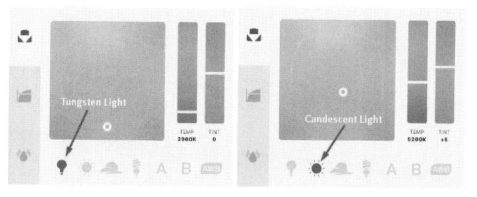

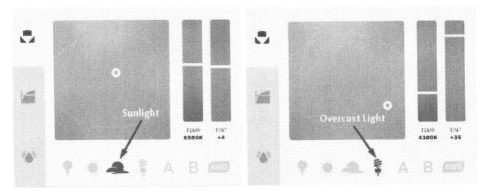

Selecting 'Automatic White Balance' (AWB) automatically changes the white balance as you move from one scene to another or from one light source to another. It is recommended if you are shooting cinematic footage to leave it at AWB. Double-tap on AWB to lock the white balance on a selected color temperature and tint setting. The Automatic White Balance (AWB) button turns red when it is locked in.

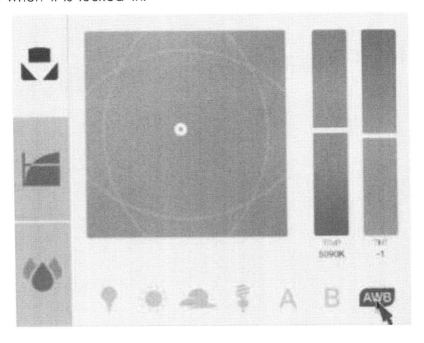

Setting Gamma

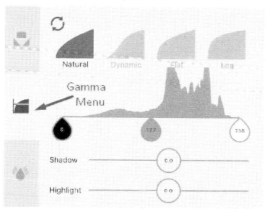

The Gamma tab is used to select the gamma and coding curve. The 'Natural' is the default iPhone Gamma curve, while the 'Dynamic,' 'Flat' and 'Log' are custom curves intended to give more image flexibility in post-production. It is a good recommendation to use the Log gamma profile if you are doing cinematic effects. So lock the Auto White Balancing in and the film in Log version. Log desaturates the picture in the background and is ideal for Post-editing.

Color Menu

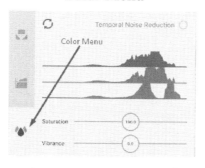

The color menu or tab gives you control over individual RGB channels, saturation, and vibrance.

71

Exposure and Focus Control

On the FiLMiC Pro viewfinder, we have two reticles, the circle reticle, which indicates the exposure (the brightness of your shot), and the square reticle indicates the focus. Drag around the circle to expose the object, then tap on it to lock it. Drag and drop the square on any object you want to focus your lens on and tap on it to lock it on the object. The circle and square reticles appear white when unlocked but red when locked to an object or subject. Locking the circle reticle on an object is ideal for shooting professional-looking videos because you don't want the light to be constantly changing and automatically adjust as you move your camera around—double-tap on the square reticle to put it in fully automatic mode. In automatic mode, the square reticle automatically focuses on an object placed in front of the camera. You can also do the same for the exposure reticle if you want it to be fully automatic. You can also lock the focus and exposure reticle in place even when it is in automatic mode to give you an overall contrast and focus quality. Double-clicking on them will deactivate that fully automatic mode.

Manual Controls

72

Open the manual controls by tapping the round icon on the bottom-left of the screen. This will open up the manual exposure dial will appear on the left, and the focus zoom dial will appear on the right. Use the exposure dial to set specific ISO and tap to lock it. Once the ISO is locked, you can use the dial to vary the shutter speed. If the Live imagery analysis tools are active, you will see zebra lines when you adjust your shutter speed, indicating when areas of an image are overexposed. You can set your focus point by adjusting the focus dial manually.

Recording Videos on the Filmic Pro

To record videos, tap the record button on the lower right part of the screen.

You can also stop recording by tapping on the same button. Next to the record button are audio bars, which indicate how loud the volume coming through is.

Volume bar

It gives you the reassurance that your audio is working when recording a video.

Playback & Clip Menu

Tap the play button next to the record button to open the FiLMiC library. Here you will be able to scroll through all of your recorded clips. Tap on a clip to open it for playback and editing. There are various editing tools on the FiLMiC Pro. E.g., the scissors tool, image adjustment sliders, downsample tool, share tool, and the Save tool.

Scissors Tool

The scissors tool allows you to trim a video clip, and it saves both the trimmed and the original clips.

Image Adjustment Tool

The image adjustment sliders allow you to make adjustments to exposure, contrast, white balance, saturation, and tint.

Any adjustments made are saved as a new clip along with the original clip.

The Downsample Tool

The downsampling tool allows you to reduce the size and quality of the clip. You can downsample your clips to any bitrate and file size.

Downsample Clip?

Downsampling will reduce the bitrate and file size of the clip.

540p

720p

1080p

Cancel

Both the downsampled and the original clips are saved.

Share tool

You can share your clip to a specific target app or copy it to a camera roll

Save Tool

Tap the save tool to save edited clip to the FiLMiC Pro folder in the photo library

However, to delete a clip from the FiLMiC Pro Library, swipe it to the left. The select clip tool ☑ is used for selecting specific clips to either upload, copy to camera roll, upload to a specific target or delete. To save selected clips to camera roll, tap on the 'save to camera roll' button to either copy a clip in camera roll or transfer to camera roll

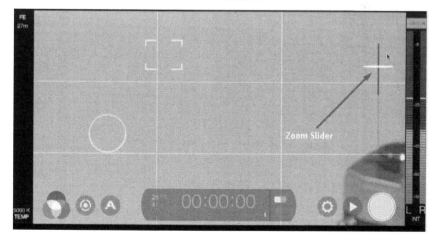

How to save from FiLMiC Pro to the Camera Roll

1. Tap to open the FiLMiC Library.

2. Tap the multi-clip selector button.

3. Tap each clip you want to save to the Camera Roll to add it to the selection (turns green)

4. Tap the Save to Camera Roll button.

5. Your clips will be copied to the Photos app.

6. Wait until all selected clips turn red which indicates the transfer has completed.

Zoom Slider

The Zoom slider on the screen allows you to control zoom in or out on objects or subjects. While zooming, you would find a little indicator changing from green to red. This shows what is happening to the quality of the image while you are zoom in. When using the zoom slider, ensure it is kept within the green zone, and you won't lose quality in your filming.

FiLMiC Remote

If you find yourself recording your videos using the rear camera of the iPhone with no one around to assist you with monitoring if everything is going as planned, then you need to install the FiLMiC Remote App on a secondary iOS Device or an iPad. With this, you can mirror your primary phone on the secondary device, and it helps you monitor your recordings remotely. You can remotely turn ON recording, zoom, adjust focus, exposure, etc. Aside from the FiLMiC Remote, you can use an App called REFLECTOR to achieve this.

Camera Plus/Pro Camera App

The Camera Plus or Pro Camera App is an alternative to the FiLMiCPro App for advanced photography. Like the FiLMiC Pro, it provides full manual mode, which enables users to control ISO, exposure, shutter speed manually as opposed to the camera app doing all that for you. You can download either the Camera plus or Pro Camera App but we recommend the Pro Camera App because it gives you full manual control over your camera as if you are using a DSLR camera.

At the bottom of the Pro Camera app, you have the exposure meter which enables you to change the exposure by sliding it either left or right. This makes the picture brighter or darker based on your needs.

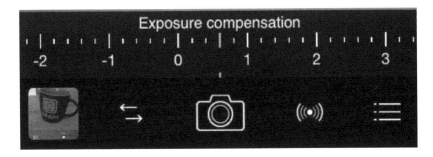

When you tap on the Pro Camera Settings Menu, you have several options:

ISO & Shutter Speed: With this, you can control the ISO and shutter speed of the camera manually. Displayed at the top of the

ISO & Shutter speed window are Shutter speed, exposure value and the ISO value. Tap on each to make individual adjustments manually and then take a photo after that. Other manual settings you can do with the pro camera app ure focus lock, select different grids, adjust tiltmeter (this shows you how leveled your camera is), etc.

Rapid Fire: Rapid Fire is used for taking burst photographs.

Anti-Shake: The Anti-Shake function help maintain a level of camera stability when taking photographs or shooting videos.

Grids: This adds or remove grid lines on the viewfinder.

Techniques to Shooting Cinematic Videos

There are several awful recordings shot using the iPhone 11, and this is because people are shooting this footage with the belief they can't get much out from a phone's cameras. You can get the best result out of the iPhone 11's camera and shoot videos like a filmmaker. You can also add some cinematic effects on your videos in several ways. To achieve this, you would need to preplan your shot rather than just holding your camera up to your face and just pointing at what you are recording. You need to get out of that mentality of always having the phone at eye level to record videos. As soon as you break that mentality, you will start getting different results with your phone that looks more cinematic.

A cinematic shot takes into consideration the necessary details within the environment of the subjects. For instance, you can record someone skateboarding using cinematic techniques. To do this, you don't just focus on the skateboarder; you need to come up with some unique techniques to make the video exciting to whoever will view it. Shooting such footage requires some level of preparation and here are some tips that will help you;

- Take into consideration the environment of the skateboarder like the trees, cars, and buildings around.
- Focus your camera on the road and allow him to ride into the scene from behind,
- Zoom in on one of the skateboard wheels while in motion

- Shoot some super slow-motion mode on the wheels by setting the camera to record in SLO-MO mode at 1080p 240 fps.
- Carry out some color adjustments while shooting.
- Apply a warped speed effect by zooming into the subject from the opposite direction.

Now, here are some cinematic techniques on the Camera App to help you achieve the above points:

Shoot Manually

To get more control of your camera for cinematic shots, you need to film manually. Deactivate all automation, whether you are using an App or not. This gives you complete control of all cameras. Manual control gives you absolute control of your focus, enabling you to use a shallow depth of field. Depth of field is when things are in the background out of focus, and things are in the fore-ground in focus verse versa. Getting objects in focus and out of focus gives your video that cinematic look. You can get the camera close to focus on your subject. This is useful when focusing your cameras on the skateboard wheel. You don't have enough control when you are in the Auto Settings.

Applying B-Roll

You will need to shoot a lot of B-rolls at the beginning of the video. Do a bottom-up B-Roll shoot at the beginning of the foot-age to give your viewers a sense of the scene, setting the tone for the footage. B-Roll gives the viewers an idea of the subject's environment, thereby telling a story. In other words, B-Roll is that extra footage that gives you a look into what is going on around a specific subject. In other words, the B-Roll is that added footage that enhances the story so that your viewers become more engaged with the content that you are creating. It is that extra-wide shot, drone shots, or slow-Mo shots of the subject in his environment.

Why do you need a B-Roll?

B-Roll is important because it tells a visual story. It breaks up your video and keeps it interesting in a top-down approach. For instance, you have seen movie scenes, where the movie begins with a super-wide shot of a city.

Then it is zoomed in a little bit and the city becomes a little bit closer.

Then you have an overhead shot with some traffic underneath and the camera settles down to a neighborhood before resting on a front door or in the front of a building.

And finally, the camera ends up inside a house where the actors are. This is what a top-down approach to B-Roll is all about.

Professionally shot B-Rolls can be sold on different stock footage platforms like www.shutterstock.com/video for as much as $20 and up to $100 is you are selling 4k clips. This is a cool way to make some income from your iPhone.

Tips for Shooting Enhanced B-Roll footage

For you to get B-Roll done for your cinematic shoot, here are some tips that can help you:

- <u>Plan the Shoot:</u> Study the subject, go to the location to make a note and visualize what you intend to shoot. This gives you an idea of what to do and where to do it when shooting the scene.

- Shoot your B-Roll at 24 frame per second to get that Cinematic feel.

- <u>Stabilize your video:</u> This means you will need to mount the iPhone on a tripod or a Gimbal for more stabile videos.

- <u>Take a variety of B-Roll shots</u>: Shoot around the subject, shoot high, shoot low, shoot wide, shoot medium, shoot up close etc. The more attractive you make your shots the more engaging your audience will be when they are watching your video.
- <u>Be creative:</u> Use a time lapse, hypo lapse, use slow motion, speed things up, speed ramp things. These are tools at your disposal that make your B-Roll interesting.

Color adjustments while shooting

You can adjust color exposures during filming with the aid of the FiLMiC Pro App preset. With Filmic Pro Preset, set up a variety of white balance color temperate and tints and save them. During video recording, switch between the preset color settings. Changing colors during filming prevents you from just shooting an overly saturated and overly contrasted clip. It gives you an option or log profile to color grade your footage. Apple has done very well to merge the color temperatures in all three lenses of the iPhone 11 pro max, so there isn't too much shift on the white balance as you switch lenses, which is one of the problems all smart-phones with multiple lenses have.

Adding a warped speed effect to your filming

To add a warped speed effect to the skateboard footage, during recording, bring up the zoom wheel, and while approaching the subject slowly, turn the zoom wheel in the opposite direction. When this is done correctly, it gives the recording a warped speed effect. Applying the warp speed effect does not require any app, just the zoom wheel.

Camera Movement

Camera movement is very important when filming cinematic videos. Take control of the camera by finding different ways to get a unique perspective or angular shots of your subject. You may be high looking down, down looking up, etc. It would be best if you found your environment to see where you can keep your phone to get a different perspective on your subject. To achieve this, you can fix your camera on a motorized slider, a gimbal, or a drone to get some ariel shots. Ensure the camera is moved in a slow methodical and thought out movements. You can also get a bottom-up coverage of the subject by filming from the ground or lawn and ensure the grass appears on the viewscreen.

Using External Lenses

Try different external lenses. For instance, to shoot the wheels of the skateboard while in motion, you use a wide-angle external lens. There are various elements you can add to your lens that changes the overall feel and look of the footage.

Audio Zoom Effect

This is integrated into the iPhone 11 camera by Apple. The ways it works is simple, whenever you are recording, pinch out on the viewfinder to zoom in towards a subject creating sound and the sound becomes clearer. You could get better audio quality by plugging in an external microphone.

Video Editor

You can do a lot of pro editing with the video editor on the iPhone 11, 11 Pro and 11 Pro Max. A key thing to note is that the video editing done on the iPhone 11 series video editor app are non-destructive. This means every change made to the video can be undone in reverse order. You have a full assortment of adjust tools with which to play around. You can trim, rotate, change vertical/horizontal tilt, flip, change aspect ratio (original, freeform, square 16:9, 10:8, 7:5, 4:3 etc), switch between portrait/landscape, turn Sound ON or Mute a video. You can also go into the editing interface, just like the photo editor and change the values of the effects. For instance, you can adjust the video's exposure, highlights, adjust shadows, saturation, vibrance, definition, vignette, sharpness, etc. You can also add filters and like the photo editing, you can adjust the intensity of the individual filters for the videos

About the Author

 Derrick Richard is a tech geek with several years of experience in the ICT industry. He passionately follows latest tech trends and his passion is in figuring out the solution to complex problems.

Derrick holds a Bachelor and a Master's Degree in ICT respectively from Georgetown University, Washington DC. He lives in Sara-sota, Florida.

Printed in Great Britain
by Amazon